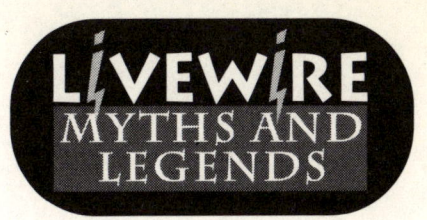

The Pied Piper

re-told by
Philip Page

Published in association with
The Basic Skills Agency

Hodder & Stoughton

A MEMBER OF THE HODDER HEADLINE GROUP

Acknowledgements
Cover: Doug Lewis
Illustrations: Philip Page

Orders: please contact Bookpoint Ltd, 78 Milton Park, Abingdon, Oxon OX14
4TD. Telephone: (44) 01235 827720, Fax: (44) 01235 400454. Lines are open
from 9.00 – 6.00, Monday to Saturday, with a 24 hour message answering
service. Email address: orders@bookpoint.co.uk

British Library Cataloguing in Publication Data
A catalogue record for this title is available from The British Library

ISBN 0 340 80010 0

First published 2001
Impression number   10 9 8 7 6 5 4 3 2 1
Year   2007 2006 2005 2004 2003 2002 2001

Copyright © 2001 Philip Page

Typeset by SX Composing DTP, Rayleigh, Essex
Printed in Great Britain for Hodder & Stoughton Educational, a division of
Hodder Headline Plc, 338 Euston Road, London NW1 3BH by Athenaeum
Press, Gateshead, Tyne & Wear.

The Pied Piper

Contents

1	Hamelin	1
2	The Pied Piper	4
3	The River Weser	11
4	The Broken Promise	16
5	The Hill and the Cave	20
6	The Silent Street	24

1

Hamelin

Up until the start of the year 1294
Hamelin was a peaceful little town in
Germany.
There was nothing unusual about the place,
or the people who lived there.
But in the year 1294 some very
unusual things happened there.
The first unusual thing was the rats.

In the spring of 1294
there were rats everywhere!
People had never seen so many.
Of course, there had always been
some rats in Hamelin,
but now there were thousands and
thousands of them.

The farmers were the first to notice them.
They got into the barns and ate all the corn.
When that was gone the rats moved on.
They went into the big storehouses
in the town.
Soon, they had eaten all the food
in there as well.
That was when the real trouble began.

The rats began to look for food in the houses.
They went everywhere.
They went in the kitchens and ate the bread.
They went in the bedrooms
and ate the straw mattresses.
They even ate the thatched roofs!

The people of Hamelin were angry
and frightened.
What if the rats attacked the children?
What if they brought horrible diseases?

Something had to be done.

2

The Pied Piper

The Mayor of Hamelin called a meeting
of the town council.
'We have got to get rid of the rats,' he said.
'We know that,' said one of the
town councillors, 'but how?'

The Mayor turned to the town ratcatcher.
'Have you tried cats?' he asked.
'The rats have killed the cats,'
said the ratcatcher.

'What about using poison?'
'We've run out of poison,'
replied the ratcatcher.
'And it's dangerous,' said another councillor.
'What if a child ate it?'

Somebody suggested killing the rats
with bows and arrows.
Everybody laughed.
The meeting went on for hours.
Nobody could think of a way
to get rid of the rats.

Just then there was a knock on the door.
'See who that is,' said the Mayor.
'Tell them to go away. We're busy.'
But then the door opened.
In stepped a very strange looking person.

They could not believe their eyes.
In front of them stood a tall, thin man.
His pale blue eyes sparkled
and there was a smile on his lips.
But it wasn't his face that was strange.
It was his clothes.
They were all different colours.

The Mayor was the first to speak.
'What do you want?' he asked angrily.
'Can't you see we're having
an important meeting?'

'I hear you're having a problem with rats,'
said the stranger.
'What's that got to do with you?'
said the Mayor.

'I can get rid of them,' said the man.
'Oh, so you're a ratcatcher?'
sneered the Mayor.
The stranger smiled.
'No, I don't catch rats,' he said.
'I get rid of them.'

'What's your name?' asked the Mayor.
'People call me the Pied Piper.
Pied, because of my coloured clothes,
and Piper because of this,' he said.

He moved to the middle of the room.
From the bag that hung from his shoulder
he took out a small flute.

'What do you do with that'
asked the town ratcatcher,
'play tunes to the rats?'

'That's exactly what I do,' said the stranger.
For a minute nobody could speak
for laughing.

Still the Piper smiled.
'Oh it works,' he said.
'I can get rid of all sorts of things –
rats, locusts, snakes,
spiders, ants – everything!'

The Mayor and the town council
whispered together.
Then the Mayor turned to the Pied Piper.
'What have we got to lose?
Go ahead and try.'

'And the price?' said the Piper.
'What will you pay me
when the rats have gone?'
'If you get rid of the rats, we'll give you
one thousand guilders★,' said the mayor.

★ A guilder was a gold coin.

'That's a lot of money!'
said the town ratcatcher.
'It will be worth it,' replied the mayor.

The Pied Piper smiled.
'I agree,' he said.
'One thousand guilders it is.'
He turned and left the room.

3

The River Weser

The Pied Piper went to the middle
of the town square.
He started to play his flute.
The Mayor and the town council stood
outside the town hall and watched.
'I can't hear any music,' said the Mayor.
'I knew he was a fraud,'
said the town ratcatcher.

But the rats could hear the Piper's music.
The came swarming out of the houses.
They ran down the streets to the town square.
Soon the Piper was surrounded by thousands
and thousands of rats.
The town square looked as if it was covered
by a living carpet of rats.

Still playing, the Piper started to move.
He walked slowly out of the town square.
The rats followed him.
The people of Hamelin watched
from every window.
They were amazed.

The Piper walked down the main street.
Behind him, the rats followed like a grey,
brown and black stream.
He walked out of the town
through the main gates.
The people cheered when the last rat
passed through the gates.

The Piper walked to the banks
of the River Weser close to the town.
Still playing, he walked into the water.
The rats followed.

13

The Pied Piper kept on playing.
All around him the rats drowned.
It took a long time before the river
carried away the last of the dead rats.

Then the Piper stopped playing.
He put away his flute
and got out of the river.
He went straight to the town hall.

'You owe me one thousand guilders,'
he said to the Mayor.

4

The Broken
Promise

The Mayor looked very worried.
'Could you wait outside for a minute?'
he said to the Pied Piper.

As soon as the Piper had left the room
everybody started talking.
'Where will we get one thousand guilders?'
somebody asked.
'I told you it was too much,'
said the town ratcatcher.

'Why should we pay him anything?'
said another man.
'After all, the rats have gone now.'

'That's right,' said the Mayor.
'They are dead and gone.
He can't bring them back.'
But one person was worried.
'We did make a promise to pay him,' he said.
'And so we shall,' said the Mayor.

The called the Piper back in.

'We can't afford one thousand guilders,'
the Mayor told him.
'That is not my problem,' said the Piper.
'Look,' said the Mayor,
'how about a hundred guilders?'
'We agreed on a thousand,' said the Piper.
He was not smiling any more.

The Mayor lost his temper.
'A thousand guilders is too much!'
he shouted.
'We'll give you one hundred.
Take it or leave it!'

'You promised me one thousand,'
said the Piper quietly.
'I kept my promise, now you keep yours.'

'How dare you speak to me like that!'
the Mayor yelled.
'You'll take one hundred or nothing.'

The Pied Piper turned
and walked to the door.
'I will come back for my payment,'
he said before he left.

19

5

The Hill and the Cave

The days and the weeks went by.
The people of Hamelin thought that they had
seen the last of the Pied Piper.
Then on 26 June, the Piper returned.

He was not wearing his brightly
coloured clothes.
He was dressed as a hunter.
On his head was a strange red hat.

It was early in the morning.
The Mayor and most of the adults
had gone to church.

Once again the Piper went to the town square.
He took his flute from his bag
and started to play.

Once again there was the sound
of pattering feet.
But this time it was not the rats of Hamelin
who came to him.
It was the children.

The Piper left the town square.
The children followed.
He walked through the streets
and out of the town gates.

The Piper did not go to the river.
He turned towards a tall hill.
Behind him came the children.
Some were running.
Some were skipping.
Some were holding hands.
All of them were laughing and smiling.

The Pied Piper stopped
at the bottom of the hill.
The children waited behind him.
Suddenly there was a deep rumbling sound.
The ground shook and the side of the hill
opened up.
The children gasped.
They saw a great cave in the side of the hill.

The Piper walked into the cave.
The children followed him inside.
Then the mouth of the cave closed.
The hill looked just as it had always done.

One hundred and thirty children
went into the cave with the Pied Piper.
They were never seen again!

6

The Silent Street

The people of Hamelin came out of
the church.
They wondered where all the children were.

A nurse who had been looking after a baby
told them the dreadful news.
She had followed the Piper and the children.
She had seen them go into the cave in the hill.

But not all the children of Hamelin
had disappeared.
Three children had been left behind.

One was a small boy who had run back home
to get his coat.
When he reached the hill,
all the children had gone.
Another boy had an injured leg.
He could not go as fast as the others
and had got left behind.
A little blind girl was also left behind.
She could not keep up with the others.

The people of Hamelin asked the children
about the Piper's music.
'It was beautiful,' said the little girl.
'It made me think that if I went with him
I would be able to see again.'
'And my leg would get better,' said the boy.

The boy who had gone back for his coat
burst into tears.
'All our friends have gone,' he cried.
'Why didn't the Piper wait for us?'

Hamelin became a sad town.
Nobody laughed and nobody smiled
any more.

The people of the town passed a law.
Nobody was allowed to dance or play music
in the street the children had walked down
with the Piper.
For hundreds of years afterwards
it was known as 'Silent Street'.

What happened to the lost children?
Nobody knows.
Some people believed that they were seen
again in a far away part of Europe.

And the Pied Piper?
He was never seen again.